JAN 1 3 2016

P9-BYE-116

AMAZING STRUCTURES
ROLLER COASTERS

by Rebecca Pettiford

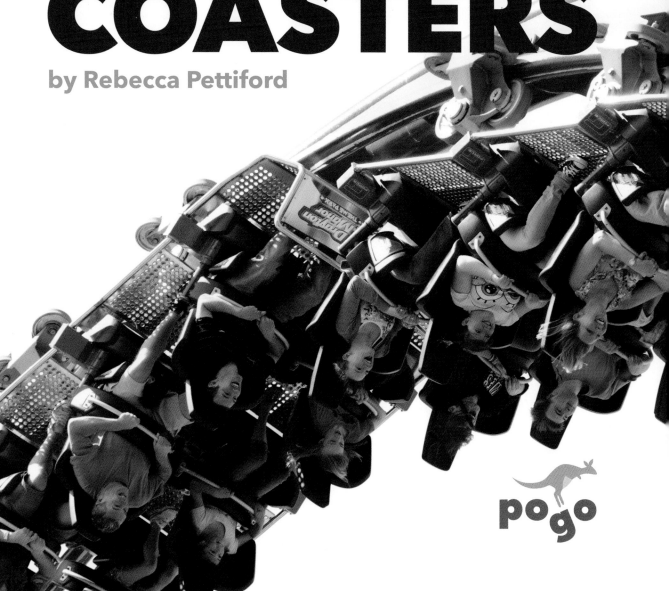

pogo

Ideas for Parents and Teachers

Pogo Books let children practice reading informational text while introducing them to nonfiction features such as headings, labels, sidebars, maps, and diagrams, as well as a table of contents, glossary, and index.

Carefully leveled text with a strong photo match offers early fluent readers the support they need to succeed.

Before Reading

- "Walk" through the book and point out the various nonfiction features. Ask the student what purpose each feature serves.
- Look at the glossary together. Read and discuss the words.

Read the Book

- Have the child read the book independently.
- Invite him or her to list questions that arise from reading.

After Reading

- Discuss the child's questions. Talk about how he or she might find answers to those questions.
- Prompt the child to think more. Ask: Have you ever ridden on a roller coaster? Did you enjoy it?

Pogo Books are published by Jump!
5357 Penn Avenue South
Minneapolis, MN 55419
www.jumplibrary.com

Copyright © 2016 Jump!
International copyright reserved in all countries. No part of this book may be reproduced in any form without written permission from the publisher.

Library of Congress Cataloging-in-Publication Data

Pettiford, Rebecca.
  Roller coasters / by Rebecca Pettiford.
     pages cm. – (Amazing structures)
  Includes index.
  ISBN 978-1-62031-215-5 (hardcover: alk. paper) –
  ISBN 978-1-62496-302-5 (ebook)
  1. Roller coasters–Juvenile literature. I. Title.
  GV1860.R64P47 2015
  791.06'8–dc23
                                    2014042538

Series Editor: Jenny Fretland VanVoorst
Series Designer: Anna Peterson
Photo Researcher: Anna Peterson

Photo Credits: ChameleonsEye/Shutterstock, 8; Corbis, 6–7; Dreamstime, 1; Getty, 9, 17; iStock, 3; jaibiru/Shutterstock.com; Shawn Wainwright/Flickr, 12–13; Shutterstock, 5, 10–11, 16, 18–19, 23; Thinkstock, cover, 4, 20–21.

Printed in the United States of America at Corporate Graphics in North Mankato, Minnesota.

TABLE OF CONTENTS

CHAPTER 1

A THRILLING RIDE

Have you ever been to an **amusement park**?

Did you ride the roller coasters?

People who ride them enjoy the thrill of fast rides. People have found ways to make fast rides for a long time.

3 0053 01161 1921

Today's roller coasters started as something much simpler: a slide.

In the 1600s, people in Russia built tall, wooden ice slides. To reach the top, people climbed stairs. They rode down the ice on a sled. Sand at the end of the slide helped them stop.

What do roller coasters look like today?

DID YOU KNOW?

The Switchback Railway was the first coaster in the United States. It opened in 1884 at Coney Island in Brooklyn, New York.

CHAPTER 2

HOW ROLLER COASTERS WORK

A roller coaster looks like a train.
A chain of open cars moves on a **track**.
A **motor** pulls each car up a hill.

Suddenly, the car drops.
It twists and turns. At times,
it may be upside down!

Starting high is a key part
of how the ride works.

By starting high, the car has the energy it needs to move. This is called **potential energy**.

As the car drops, the potential energy changes to **kinetic energy**. This energy comes from the ride's drop. It also comes from the pull of **gravity**. It's what makes the ride fast.

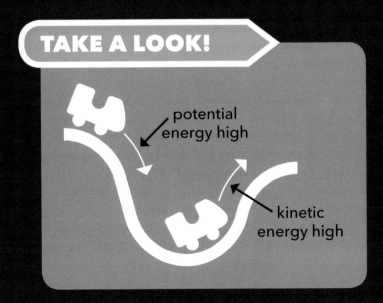

potential energy high

kinetic energy high

The Kingda Ka is the fastest coaster in North America. It reaches 128 miles per hour (206 kilometers per hour) in 3.5 seconds! It is also the tallest roller coaster in the world. At its tallest point it is 456 feet (139 meters) high!

DID YOU KNOW?

Some rides use a **launch** system to start the cars. The launch builds up and stores a lot of energy. When the energy is released, the cars zoom forward.

Kingda Ka

Roller coasters run on incredibly powerful motors.

A car's engine usually delivers about 175 **horsepower**. But roller coasters can produce nearly 21,000 horsepower!

Who makes roller coasters? Let's find out.

DID YOU KNOW?

A roller coaster needs **brakes** so it can slow down and stop when the ride ends. The brakes are built into the track.

CHAPTER 3

BUILDING ROLLER COASTERS

Designers build roller coasters. They look for new ways to make the rides faster and more fun.

Newer rides are made of steel. They are the fastest and tallest rides. They have more drops and loops.

Wooden coasters are often older and louder. They are not as tall or as fast. They do not loop, and the ride is shaky. For some riders, this is what makes a wooden roller coaster fun!

Do you like speed? Do you like thrills?

Then you like roller coasters!

Do you have a favorite?

ACTIVITIES & TOOLS

BUILD A ROLLER COASTER

You can build your own roller coaster! You will need the following materials:

- a small ball or marble
- about six feet (1.8 m) of ¾ inch (1.9 centimeters) foam pipe insulation
- scissors
- masking tape
- supports such as books or boxes
- a plastic cup

❶ Cut the tubing in half lengthwise. This will be your track. Your ball or marble will be your car.

❷ Your car will need potential and kinetic energy. You will want to place the start of your track high so the car can make it through the course.

❸ Use your tape and supports to make the starting point. You can even tape the starting point up on a wall.

❹ Include at least one loop and one hill.

❺ Place the cup at the end of the course. You will want the ball to land in the cup.

❻ Place your car at the start of the course. Let it go. Did the coaster work? If not, figure out what went wrong. Make changes and try again.

amusement park: A large outdoor area with rides and other forms of entertainment.

brakes: A device that slows or stops a moving vehicle by placing pressure on the wheels.

designer: One who creates and manufactures a new product style.

gravity: The force that pulls a body or thing toward the center of the earth or toward another body or thing.

horsepower: A unit of measurement that describes the rate at which an engine can do work.

kinetic energy: The energy that something has just by being in motion.

launch: To set in motion.

motor: A machine, usually run on electricity, that makes a vehicle move.

potential energy: The energy something gains by where it's located.

steel: A metal made from iron and carbon.

track: A continuous line of rails, which are bars made of steel or wood.

INDEX

TO LEARN MORE

Learning more is as easy as 1, 2, 3.

1) Go to www.factsurfer.com

2) Enter "rollercoasters" into the search box.

3) Click the "Surf" to see a list of websites.

With factsurfer, finding more information is just a click away.